Mother Pearl

MOTHER PEARL

Sarah
Flame

ISBN 979-8-218-53449-3

Interior artwork by Sarah Flame
Cover & Design by Tell Tell Poetry
Edited by Tell Tell Poetry

First Printing, 2024

I am dedicating this work to my editorial team at Tell Tell and my beautiful family.

CONTENTS

STUDY OF BEINGS

STUDY OF HEALING

ABOUT THE AUTHOR

INTRODUCTION

Mother Pearl was birthed from darkness. It began with my healing from a near-fatal car accident. I spent long periods of time resting my neck, allowing images and symbols to expand my imagination. My dreams were vivid, and through healing I developed a deeper relationship to my imaginal and relational life. My study of psychoanalysis and expressive arts therapy taught me that healing can occur from alchemical symbols. *Mother Pearl* is a journey back toward the nurturing aspects of maternal instinct—what holds us in times of peril. The pearl won at great price reflects our willingness to journey into the depths of the unconscious to gain a larger perspective. I begin with the symbol namaste, a greeting that stays in the heart.

In *Mother Pearl*, art and poetry are linked to create breaths in space—pauses in time that reveal layers of feeling and perception.

Mother Pearl is an exploration of art and poetry
a journey into self-love and recovery with expressive art
infusing love into a bridge of dreams and self-reflection
to reframe diverse cultural symbology
taking back power and resurrecting strength in language
giving bounty to the lush images of naturalist earth

The female embodied
speaking and dancing through form

A pearl won at great price
shining from the depths

Darkness illuminates the soul

What we see is what we cultivate

Wounds heal with time

Sweetness is remembered

All of this . . .

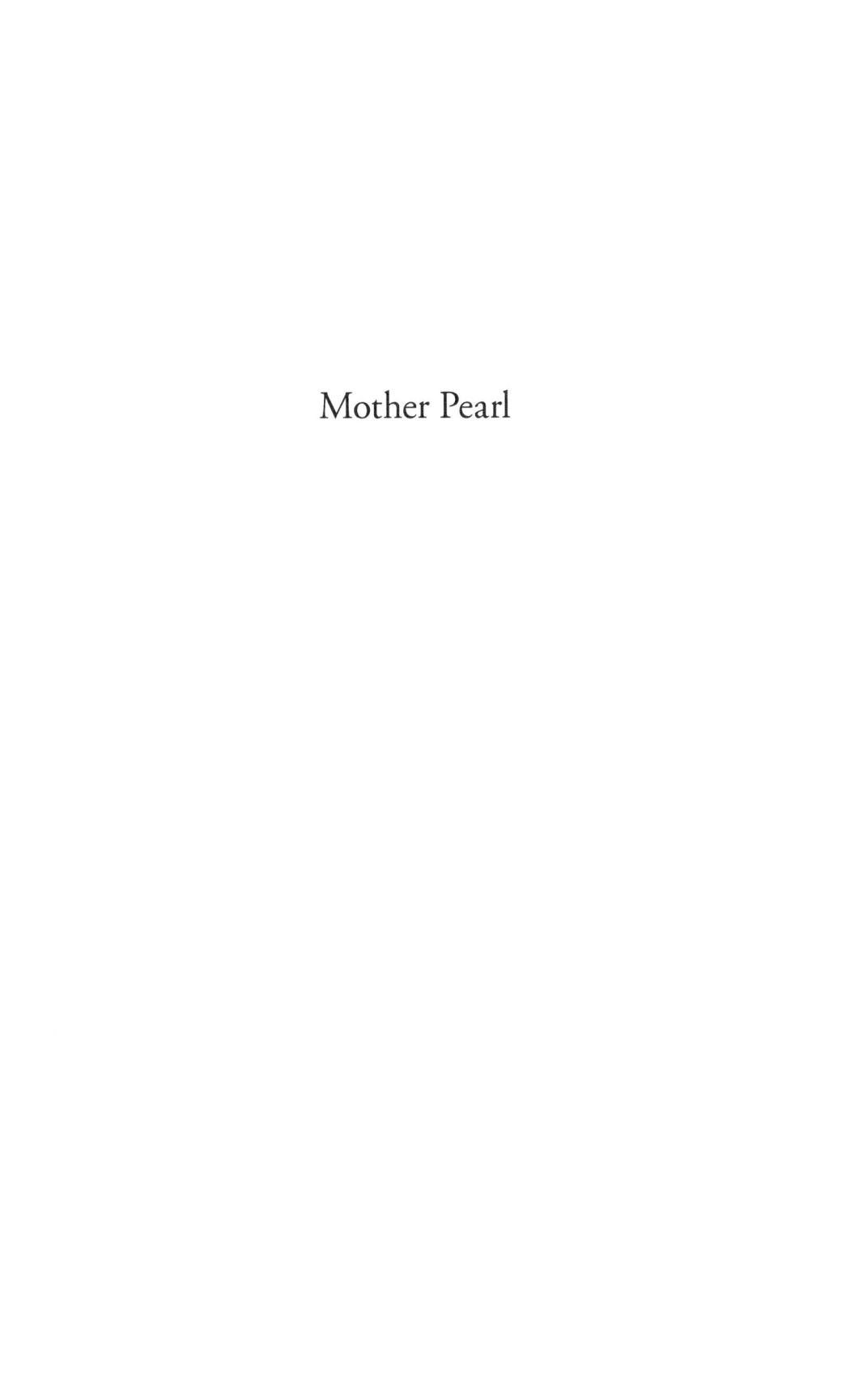

Mother Pearl

STUDY OF
LAND & SKY

IN THE LIGHT

In the beginning
a butterfly was born

From the greatest darkness
lightness can emerge

Moon Cycles

The moon glows outside my window
big enough to embrace it all

to tumble into complexity
or simplicity

I see my reflection
cries of resurrection

in darkness
toward light

MEDICINE WHEEL

I dance the four directions
in celebration of our friendship

a salt life
stretching our bodies

across waves
taking us back to shore

TURTLE ISLAND

Could be
a sacred land
that still exists
in time

MISTY

On a shore far away
Misty appeared under veils
ready to show me
what is revealed through her

SATURN

In our worst moment
you asked
what if we were on Saturn

I never liked fighting
I just wanted
to fold in your arms

like a lost bird
one wing clipped
with a desire to unfurl

SACRED HEART

I am in the desert
after losing the love of my life
blessed by painted flowers

Letting go is a bursting flame
bright red
sacré-coeur

Water washes
my sight clean

MERMAID

I might have been a mermaid
on shore
Anything is possible

I felt so alive near the ocean

With you . . .

THUNDER LADY

From cracked places
and broken bones
Thunder Lady appeared

Dancing with electricity
she told me I was going to live
to find my connection to life

VENUS

A woman's body

Is a map to wisdom

Her womb carries stars

Do not forget this . . .

AQUAMARINE

What to understand
or shed
as time passes

Anchor this moment
let it be enough
not to be missed

SURRENDER

Where my soul is embraced
after a rocky existence

STUDY OF
FLORA & FAUNA

EVERGREEN

The beauty of a
washed beginning

RAINBOW LAMB

Amidst all the fighting
Rainbow Warriors
inherit the earth

They beautifully dream
we can be one
in unity

UNICORN

Appeared as a dream guide
telling me to keep going
to remember divinity

STAG HEART

Your reign was a long winter

Spring is a new destiny

Nest

Warm

Inviting

Where birds sing

SPIRIT FEATHERS

A pair of feathers
painted in both day
and nighttime

44 SARAH FLAME

PEACOCK

I found two feathers

Empress
Translucent
Ember

These words heal

May I be respected . . .

DOVE IN HARMONY

Sounds in the universe
as tears stain your eyes

I bow

I will always see you
as a dove in harmony

FLOWERS

Can we ride bicycles together
creating peaceful roads
holding hands
not letting go
too soon

WATER LILY

In technicolor
stay true

SUNFLOWERS

Growing outside of bars
I am learning the cost of freedom

DAFFODILS

Bringing forth
bursting
heart-red

PERFUME

For all the times
I tumbled in the sheets
sweating and dirty

I now anoint myself
with peony and black currant
to rise a muddy lotus

STUDY OF
BEINGS

Amsterdam Shoes

Mother
you survived a war

Your shoes never fit

You now have boxes of shoes

So do I

THREE SPOONS

She cooked with three spoons
one for every season

The scents of food
wafted into windows

Knowing how to cook
is medicine to the earth

NOTHING TO LOSE

We have nothing to lose
crossing these tracks

I will run fast and
say your name, Sister

Behind me
you are smiling
into the wind

ESMERALDA

She stares out of amethyst eyes

Her mane dances in the wind

As she bows to her legacy

More than a horse

A guardian who protects

STARFISH

She gifted me a starfish

I will always be around you

She is an angel

Can I be hers too

EARTH GUARDIANS

We plant seeds for the future

This life is a memory of us

Vibrancy

QUEEN BEE

Scents of honeysuckle
gardenia and rose
blooming

Her sensual thighs
lips and legs

The queen bee
loves herself
unconditionally

80 SARAH FLAME

GOLDEN CREATURES

I wake up with beach hair
to the waves that soothe
all the years I decided
not to be myself

82 SARAH FLAME

APHRODITE

She who holds herself high
glistening on the edge
of a mother-of-pearl seashell

I am beauty   worthy   strong
Repeat this again

BIRTH

Glistening

A pearl won at great price
Shining from depths
Darkness illuminates the soul
What we see is what we cultivate
Wounds are healed with time
Sweetness is remembered

All of this . . .
Is the birth of a mother pearl

STUDY OF
HEALING

SPARROW

A group of branches
hold a sparrow
singing out life
to everyone

Who knows what miracle
could happen

Walk to
the other side

Hummingbird

She spends her time
looking for sweetness

Finds the center
of shortened time
expanding to infinity

Mesa Verde

We are part of an era
of mystics
of dreamers
of visionaries

Our stories will be etched in canyons
and constellations of stars

Remember us gazing next to one another

BIRD OF PARADISE

When my car collided with a tree
I saw sunbursts of color
I later saw myself

I think the most radical choice
is to love ourselves
then someone else

94 SARAH FLAME

OWL

Did I choose to see

All the blessings bestowed on me

Was that the question all along

Did time become a teacher

About the Author

Sarah Flame is a bhakti writer devoted to raising consciousness in the feminine emergence movement. Her work is rooted in an embodiment of the natural world and service to the earth. She is a postgraduate of psychoanalysis and has been in the field of holistic healing for  over twenty years. Her art and poetry are offerings and reflections toward beauty and the divine.